The Allure of the Rink
Roller Skating at the Arena Gardens, 1935-53

Sarah Webber

A publication from and in support of the
National Museum of Roller Skating
Lincoln, Nebraska

The Allure of the Rink,
Roller Skating at the Arena Gardens, 1935-53
©1999 National Museum of Roller Skating
4730 South Street, P.O. Box 6579
Lincoln, Nebraska 68506   USA
402/483-7551 ext. 16   e-mail: rllrsktmus@aol.com
http://www.usacrs.com/museum.htm

The National Museum of Roller Skating is a non-profit institution established in 1980 for the purpose of preserving and documenting the history of roller skating through the collection of artifacts, films and photographs, and library materials. The museum contains exhibits tracing the development of roller skating technology, sports, and entertainment.

The museum publishes the *Historical Roller Skating Overview*, a bi-monthly newsletter available to members, featuring historical articles and museum news. For further information about the museum and how to become a member please write to the above address.

ISBN 0-9658192-1-3

CONTENTS

A C K N O W L E D G E M E N T S

While in my first months at the National Museum of Roller Skating, I came across numerous photographs from the Arena Gardens in Detroit, Michigan. I kept coming across photographs, year books, newsletters, and many more items from the rink, and, my curiosity increasing, realized that the artifacts told a larger story than of just one roller rink. Existing from the mid 1930s through the mid 1950s, the Arena Gardens came to symbolize these decades, a time when thousands of Americans embraced roller skating at the rink as a significant social and recreational activity. I became further interested in this rink as a symbol for what I came to call "America's Rink Era" upon discovering that few roller skating histories exist; indeed, few histories even mention roller skating when discussing the history of American popular culture and American sports. Roller skating provides a rich, largely untapped historical subject with which to explore American popular culture, society, and sport, particularly but not exclusively of working class Americans, of which I hope my book is but a start.

There are many I wish to thank for their help with this book. First, I want to thank Michael Zaidman, Director & Curator of the National Museum of Roller Skating, who, though initially shocked by the size of my history of the Arena Gardens, decided it would make a good book for the museum to publish. George Pickard, Executive Director of USA Roller Skating, Treasurer of the National Museum of Roller Skating Board of Trustees, and a former Arena Gardens roller skater, agreed after reading the manuscript. I want to thank both of them for publishing what became my favorite subject while working at the museum.

My appreciation also goes to the museum Board of Trustees for their support: Bert Anselmi-President, Chester Fried-Vice-President,

George Pickard-Secretary/Treasurer, Annelle Anderson, Robert Bollinger, Frank Cernik, Marvin Facher, Charlotte Groves, Mills Lynn, Katherine McDonell, Gordon Van Roekel, Charles Wahlig, Edmund Young, and Trustee Emeritus' Michael Brooslin, James Turner, Scott Addison Wilhite, and Assistant Curator Susan Curtis. The many members of the National Museum of Roller Skating, also made this publication possible. The contributions they have made, whether monetary or through the donation of historical artifacts and archival materials, have been vitally important in making the museum a success.

The museum wishes to thank Jeanette Tupe and Michael Zaidman, for their many extra efforts to secure the design and layout of this book. Also a sincere thank you to USA Roller Skating for their continued support of the museum.

Additionally, I want to thank my parents, Anne and Ivan Webber, and my friends Rachel Jorgenson and Erin Taylor, all of who helped edit the book and provided helpful suggestions from miles away. I also want to thank Spike Eickholt for his recommendations as well as support at home.

I wish to especially express my thanks to Fred Martin's children: Marjorie Martin McLauchlen, who recently passed away; Roland A. Martin; and especially Rose L. Martin. Rose supplied many of the specific details found here as well as proofread to make sure I had my facts straight. All three greatly assisted me by generously sharing their memories of growing up at the Arena Gardens. I also want to thank the former Arena Gardens roller skaters who shared their memories: Warren and Jewel Bowman, Peter C. Breniser, William L. Martin, Louise Silver, and Margaret Williams Walker. Without their recollections, I doubt this book would be half as interesting.

Sarah Webber,
March 1999

Robert Martin and a crowd of children from the Saturday afternoon Children's Safety Skating Club outside the Arena Gardens waiting to go inside for the masquerade Halloween party in 1938.

INTRODUCTION

Roller Skating in America

As children, Americans learned to roller skate in the 1930s, went to skate dancing classes as teenagers in the 1940s, and met their future spouses at rink refreshment counters in the 1950s. Students met at the local rink on Saturday afternoons. Children dressed up for rink Halloween parties. Women and men found it relaxing after work to skate awhile at their favorite roller rink, in the company of friends. Couples often went roller skating on first and subsequent dates. During World War II, those in the service roller skated for free.

With the advent of shortened working hours in the early twentieth century, the amount of time available to Americans for leisure increased. Along with good pay and an increase in families owning cars, millions of Americans spent their new leisure time participating in group recreational and sport activities. Beginning in the 1930s, increasing numbers of Americans went out to play, with sports and recreational activities gaining enthusiasm among both youth and adults. Americans embraced sports as a valuable way to spend their leisure time in the years between the two world wars and following the second world war. From the 1930s through the 1950s, millions of Americans spent their increased leisure time at roller rinks.

Halloween at the Arena Gardens in 1944, Fred Martin presenting a prize to a contestant.

Though roller skating enjoyed its first surge in popularity in the late 19th century, the sport hit upon rough times in the early twentieth century as a few poorly managed rinks gave rink roller skating an unsavory image. Many owners allowed their rinks to become meeting places for individuals of poor reputations who showed little respect for their fellow roller skaters. However unjustly, all rinks became tainted with the reputation of housing difficult, loud, and sometimes dangerous male teenagers, thus creating the image of rink skating as unsafe, potentially dangerous, and unwholesome.

With only an estimated one hundred and fifty rinks open in 1910, many rink owners and managers began working on creating a more upscale, uniform image of roller rinks. In the mid 1930s, seventeen rink operators, who had individually been cleaning up their own rinks, organized to improve upon the low regard many Americans held for roller rinks. They encouraged rinks that catered to working and middle class families' social need for a safe, clean, and enjoyable recreation space. Roller skating once again emerged as one of America's favorite indoor sports and social recreations in the 1930s, ranking as the second most popular participant sport after bowling. Popularity for the indoor sport boomed, and Americans bought three times as many roller skates as ice skates in the 1930s. Millions of Americans embraced rink roller skating in the 1930s, and by 1942 more than 3,000 rinks existed in the United States with over ten million Americans roller skating in them. Articles citing the new boom appeared in *Time* and *Life*. In 1941, *Newsweek*

The Arena Gardens decorated for Christmas.

reported that "youngsters in droves have been discovering the possibilities of dancing on maple wheels." And while millions roller skated, for hundreds of thousands of Americans skating at the local roller rink became an intimate part of their lives. The rinks often became as popular as roller skating itself, with many rinks gaining fame across the United States.

The Arena Gardens in Detroit, Michigan, acquired such eminence. Noted across the country for its professional staff, skating clubs, building features, organist, and even its refreshment counter, the Arena Gardens quickly attained a legendary status after it opened in 1935. While admired for being one of the largest rinks in the country, the Arena Gardens also gained fame for its management, embodied by general manager Fred Martin, one of the vanguard rink operators who worked to clean up roller rink skating's image. From 1935 until it closed in 1953, the Arena Gardens captured the loyalty of both the people of Detroit and of the thousands of Americans who visited. This celebrated roller rink, so completely designed and organized around providing roller skaters with a wholesome and enjoyable experience, represented then, as now, the paragon rink in the era of roller rink skating in the United States.

Detroit in the 1930s & the Opening of the Arena Gardens
In the 1930s, Detroit boasted a population of over a million and a half people, with large immigrant populations from Poland, the Ukraine, Germany, Italy, Russia, Greece, Hungary, Syria, and substantial numbers from Ireland, China, and Mexico. Detroit, the fourth largest city in the United States in absolute population, reigned as the third largest in the number of foreign born in the United States. Moreover, the Great Migration during and after the First World War brought thousands of southern African Americans to Detroit, increasing in population from 5,700 in 1910 to over 150,000 by the end of the Depression. The vast increase in the city's population following the turn of the century resulted directly from the need for labor by the Detroit automobile industry,

The Roller Skating Rink Operators Association, RSROA
Along with managing the huge Arena Gardens, Fred Martin
helped organize and promote the sport of roller skating. In
1937, during a speed skating meet at the Arena Gardens,
Martin invited sixteen other rink operators to lunch down the
street to discuss regulating future competitions and promotion
of the sport. On April 4, 1937, over lunch at the Casa Loma
Restaurant, the seventeen men representing twenty-three rinks
across six states founded the Roller Skating Rink Operators
Association in an effort to organize roller skating through
organizing rink operators. The group elected Victor Brown, a
rink owner in Newark, New Jersey, to serve as the fledgling
association's first president, and Martin became secretary-
treasurer. All seventeen men donated one dollar to start the
organization, which Martin took back to his office at the Arena
Gardens. A single drawer in his desk became the first office
of the RSROA. Though originally small, by Thanksgiving of
that year membership reached over one hundred, and members
began holding conferences to standardize the rules of
competitive roller skating as well as rink operating procedures.
Here Fred Martin sits at his desk and the first desk of the
RSROA around 1940.

which, by the late 1930s, made three-fifths of the world's automobiles.

The Great Depression came quite suddenly to Detroit, following an era of fantastic prosperity. In 1930, following a boom year that capped off an incredibly prosperous decade in the industry, auto production plummeted. During the worst part of the Depression, around two-thirds of those previously employed in the automobile industry lost work. One third of the total labor force in the city in early 1933 was unemployed. Having reached the lowest point of the Depression, the economy both nationally and locally began to improve, with 1936 marking the second most profitable year in the history of American business. Recovery filtered down to those working in the plants, and as more people returned to full-time work, more bought automobiles. Detroit's suffering economy and citizens began to work and hope again, for just as Detroit felt the effects of the Depression early on, it was also one of the first cities to feel the recovery. A nation hungry for cars bought automobiles, and in 1936 the auto industry produced over four million cars and trucks.

Although the Depression adversely affected Americans' economic security, it proved a boon to sports. Millions, out of work or under worked, turned to inexpensive amusement through recreational and sporting activities to relive their stress in the early 1930s. Roller skating, an activity that served this function, flourished. Sports promoters and entrepreneurs responded by converting old barns and warehouses into roller rinks, and portable rinks traveled the United States, particularly the South and the Midwest, making the sport available to both small and large towns. While many aspects of American life were adversely affected by the Great Depression,

The Junior Skating Club around 1940, sitting outside the Arena Gardens where Monday night wrestling took place.

sports, and particularly roller skating, escalated in popularity across the United States.

During the early 1930s, Adam Weismuller, a former wrestler and sports enthusiast, invested heavily in an abandoned ice hockey rink. Following an accident that forced him to retire from wrestling, Weismuller turned to sports promotion and acquired the abandoned ice hockey rink in the early 1930s to hold wrestling meets. Cluttered with old benches and refuse, Weismuller cleaned and restored the building to turn it into a profitable wrestling center. His careful, imaginative promoting proved lucrative, and he quickly expanded the Arena Gardens to include other sports as well, renting the building to boxing promoters.

The Fred Martin Challenge poster offered by his manager, Joseph Munch, from the Riverview Skating Palace, Milwaukee, Wisconsin. Munch challenged any speed skater in the world for a race or series of races, from 1 mile to 100 miles against Martin, the World's 24 Hour Champion Speed Skater.

Not content with spectator sports and wanting to keep the building open throughout the week as well as tap into the popularity of roller skating, Weismuller visualized using the large Arena Gardens as a roller rink. Weismuller called upon the general manager of Chicago's popular White City Rink, Fred Martin, for advice on establishing his building as a roller rink. Martin recalled meeting with Weismuller at Trafton's Restaurant in Detroit, and "over a good bowl of pea soup," they negotiated a transaction that, according to Martin, resulted in "one of the foremost, finest, largest and most modern rinks in the United States."

Though born in 1892 in Genoa, Italy, shortly after his birth the Martin

A young Fred Martin surrounded by his staff at a Milwaukee rink around 1915.

family moved to the United States and Fred Martin grew up in San Francisco. While still a youth, he began working at a nearby rink, where he swept and sometimes played the organ. After work, Martin practiced speed skating and began competing while still in his teens, winning the Pacific Coast Championship shortly after he started competing. In 1910, his first child, Robert, was born and soon afterwards the young Martin family moved east. While not winning every race, he remained the World's Long Distance Champion Speed Skater until the early 1920s, when he gave up competitive roller skating to focus his career in rink management.

Eager to leave his management position at the White City Rink, which fell on economic hard times during the Depression, the forty-two year old Martin moved in the late summer of 1935 to Detroit to become the Arena Gardens Manager. Accompanied by his wife and five children, aged seven to twenty-five, Martin immediately began establishing the Gardens as a premiere roller rink. One of his daughters, Marjorie, recalling her first impression of the rink, stated that it reminded her of a "big, gray barn."

The Arena Gardens was large, not only to a thirteen year old but also to the adults refurbishing it. Covering an entire city block, the

Fred Martin and an unidentified man standing outside the White City Rink, Chicago, Illinois, the rink Martin managed before he moved to the Arena Gardens.

Arena Gardens loomed over the corner of Woodward Avenue and Antoinette Street. In its vicinity, tree-shaded neighborhoods with old homes converted into apartments housed business people as well as many young artists and students. Located on one of Detroit's four major arteries about three miles from downtown, the Arena Gardens was in the mid-city hub of Detroit. Beautiful residential neighborhoods, as well as cultural and economic areas of importance in the city, surrounded the Arena Gardens. Indeed, the *Detroit News* measured the importance of events in the 1930s and 1940s by the yardstick, "how close is it to Woodward Avenue?" Within the Arena Gardens neighborhood stood the Art Center with its broad lawns and marble buildings. The Main Public Library, as well as the Detroit Children's Museum, were within walking distance, as was Wayne State University, the sixteenth largest university in the United States in 1938 with over 10,000 students. Businesses within walking distance included small shops, as well as the General Motors Building, one of the largest office buildings in the United States in 1940.

The Martins assisted Weismuller in creating what became the fourth largest rink in the country, painting the building and finally installing a top grade Michigan maple floor, the best possible flooring for roller skaters. Son Roland Martin recalls laying the beautiful maple, placed over the existing concrete floor hailing from the Arena Gardens' earlier days as an ice rink. The maple boards which covered the concrete floors "were bent into a full 180 degree turn at the ends of the rink so that skaters' wheels were always following the grain of the wood," Roland remembers. Weismuller invested nearly $50,000 into restoring and updating the building before satisfied with its condition as a roller rink. Fred Martin later noted that Weismuller "risked thousands of dollars" in establishing the Arena Gardens as a skating rink, backed largely by the belief that Detroit needed "just such a place."

Not two years passed, however, before tragedy struck the rink with the death of Adam Weismuller. Following Weismuller's early death at the age of thirty-eight, his widow, Marie Weismuller, along with Martin, wrestling matchmaker Ed Lewis, and the Arena Gardens legal counsel, James Duffy, formed the Weismuller Sports Enterprises Corporation to oversee management of the rink. Each member assumed responsibility for part of the Arena Gardens. Though

Mrs. Marie Weismuller, widow of Arena Gardens proprietor Adam Weismuller.

the corporation officially oversaw management for the duration of the Arena Gardens' existence, Fred Martin ran the day-to-day operation and, in effect, controlled the roller rink.

An Enjoyable Experience

Before Weismuller's unexpectedly early death, Martin began to transform the rink towards its legendary status with his personal touch. By hiring roller skating professionals to teach the art of the sport and by seeing that all visitors at the rink enjoyed themselves, Martin changed the Arena Gardens into a sanctuary for the people of Detroit. Gambling flourished as the most popular entertainment in the city during the mid 1930s, with few family recreational activities in existence beyond the movies or sporting events such as the much beloved Detroit Tigers. When Martin first came to the Arena Gardens, he reportedly spent a great deal of time "weeding out the undesirable elements that had been hanging around the rink," barring their entrance to the new Arena Gardens. Martin moved quickly to avoid gaining an unsavory reputation, common to many rinks still at this time, at the Arena Gardens. According to Martin, a "roller skating rink should be a healthful recreational center where the graceful and exhilarating sport can be enjoyed on the highest plane."

Fred Martin worked diligently to create and maintain the Arena Gardens as such a center, and people responded to his efforts by flocking to the Arena Gardens from across the city and later the nation. Louise Silver roller skated at the Arena Gardens in the early 1950s. She recalls feeling that Martin seemed "genuinely interested in all the skaters, and would often stroll down the aisles smiling, nodding, waving to the skaters and occasionally stopping for a chat." Martin and his children, who worked with their father at the rink, "ran a tight ship and it showed," remembers William L. Martin, who skated at the Arena Gardens in the early 1940s. With rigid but good-natured discipline, Fred Martin ensured that every part of the rink, from the respectful staff to the cleanliness of the club locker rooms to the milkshakes served at the refreshment counter, all sparkled with pride to ensure roller skaters a safe and an enjoyable experience.

Eileen Ashenbrenner and William Martin in the lobby of the Arena Gardens, December 1946.

Skaters stand aside and watch professional instructors at the
Arena Gardens in the late 1930s. Notice the circles painted
on the rink floor as guides for figure skating.

CHAPTER ONE
SKATING AT THE RINK

In his effort to make the Arena Gardens a safe and enjoyable rink for the working and middle class families of Detroit, Martin turned away rowdy individuals seeking admission into the rink, as well as those with alcohol on their breaths. Moreover, the doorman only admitted individuals dressed formally and in accordance with the dress rules of the rink. In addition to observing the dress code, Martin expected his patrons to behave civilly. Once in the rink, those who insisted on roller skating fast or cutting off other skaters were asked to leave. Martin often pulled ill-behaved individuals aside to talk in his office before ejecting them from the Arena Gardens.

People across Detroit responded to Martin's disciplined efforts at establishing the Arena Gardens as a safe and enjoyable recreational facility. By 1940, approximately six thousand people skated at the Arena Gardens

Six lines of skaters dancing during a skating session at the Arena Gardens.

Four women in the Arena Gardens practice room around 1940.

each week during the regular skating sessions held Wednesday through Sunday, from 8 until 11:30 p.m. By the late 1930s, on any given night, five or six church groups skated at the Arena Gardens, with about fifty skaters in each group. The Arena Gardens also won the patronage of numerous parochial schools, Bible classes, and missionary societies, who booked the rink on certain nights during the week. Jesse Bell, who worked as the Arena Gardens Party Representative, in addition to his duties as the Speed Coach, was among the first rink employees in the country to solicit churches and schools to promote roller skating. When speaking before leaders of churches and youth groups, Bell presented photographs of the rink as well as testimonial letters from other church and school leaders

Roland Martin in the center of the rink, a skating session in progress with skaters circling the rink.

praising the rink. Recruiting youth and members of churches proved highly beneficial, for it helped to create a more wholesome atmosphere and reputation for roller skating at the Arena Gardens.

Arena Gardens patrons skated designated roller skating routines, such as all-skate, couples, or trio roller skating during the skating sessions. Sessions often had dance specials where everyone did the announced dance, whether it be a waltz or tango.

A group of children holding up Arena Gardens Roller Skating Club stickers and patches in 1938.

Margaret Walker, who skated at the Arena Gardens in the early 1940s, recalls there being so many people skating during the sessions "there was no room or space to fall."

Matinees, along with evening sessions and classes, rounded out the repertoire of skating periods at the Arena Gardens. Roland Martin remembers skating with his friends during the Saturday and Sunday matinees. Designed for pre-teens, the Saturday matinee lasted from 1 until 4 p.m. and included all-skate roller skating numbers, as well as couples and trio skating, and many games like Lucky Star, similar to musical chairs. People skated in one direction until the music stopped, then headed for a star inked on the maple floor. The stars, Roland remembers, "were all numbered so if they found one to stand on and the number was called they would win a prize, usually a real silver

A 'coffee and cake' morning skating session in 1944, with, standing to the left, Marge Martin McLauchlen, Elsbeth Muller, and Marge's husband Richard McLauchlen. Rose Martin is standing on the far right.

The Lidstone Tour
Joan Lidstone following an exhibition performance at the Arena Gardens in 1938. Lidstone toured the United States with her brother James Lidstone in 1938 to help popularize roller skating. Originally from Great Britain where they reigned as roller skating dance champions, the Lidstones skated in rinks across the United States in 1938. Nearly 4,000 people came out to watch them during their stop in Detroit at the Arena Gardens.

dollar." While the Saturday matinee was geared for pre-teens, the Sunday afternoon sessions were directed at teenagers and young adults, "a daytime version of the evening sessions," according to Roland Martin.

As Fred Martin worked to promote the Arena Gardens in the fall of 1935, he also sought to promote roller skating itself. In order to do so, he established the Arena Gardens Roller Skating Club for those skaters who regularly patronized the rink and participated in skating sessions. Martin formed the club with the intention of creating a "distinguished group of roller skaters that will command recognition through accomplished skating." Martin probably modeled the Arena Gardens Roller Skating Club after the White City Roller Club, the rink Martin worked at prior to the Arena Gardens that boasted one of the largest memberships in the United States. A year after its birth, the Arena Gardens Roller Skating Club claimed over two thousand members. In 1940, five thousand members of the Arena Gardens Roller Skating Club celebrated the fifth anniversary of the club designed for the casual skater without the time to spend in pursuit of the sport.

The Arena Gardens Roller Skating Club also enabled roller skaters to interact on a social level. In addition to providing exercise and recreation, roller skating was a popular social activity. Membership in the Arena Gardens Roller Skating Club was akin to membership in any other social club. Members received lower admission prices to the rink, invitations to a special club night held once a month, birthday party notices, and postcards announcing upcoming events. Members also received the monthly newsletter, the *Detroit Roller Skater*, sent to members both in Detroit and to those living in one of the fourteen countries on four continents who also belonged.

Patrons signed up for membership at the club desk in the lobby of the Arena Gardens, positioned to be the first thing a patron saw when entering the rink. Rose Martin, the youngest of Fred Martin's daughters, recalls the desk staffed by "personable women" who answered questions, took memberships, registered classes, sold skating magazines and Arena Gardens Roller Skating Club jewelry. Margaret Walker, who joined the club as an active skater as a child in the early 1940s, remembers club secretary Helen Wolds as "definitely a plus employee" for all the work she accomplished and the way she made one feel at home. And for many, the Arena Gardens was another home.

Earl and Mickey King, Lucy Shook, club secretary, and Nettie and Fred Martin standing in front of the club desk in 1950.

Fred Martin's eldest daughter Clarice
Martin, right, and Min Spencer, both
members of the floor staff in 1935.

CHAPTER TWO
STAFFING THE RINK

In 1936, the staff of the Arena Gardens consisted of twenty-five men and women, excluding the management. Martin treated all his employees with respect and kindness, his youngest daughter Rose recalls, and that respect in turn created loyalty to both Martin and the Arena Gardens. The entire staff worked diligently toward Martin's goal of providing every patron a safe and enjoyable experience. The special treatment patrons received started when they entered the Arena Gardens, where doorman William Wilson greeted and held the door open for every patron of the rink. Once inside, a female floor guard greeted the patrons and directed them to the checkroom, where they left their coats. Patrons then went to the skate room where attendants provided customers with a pair of skates, put on by the skate boys.

Martin required his staff to provide respectful, good service and to dress formally. By requiring his staff to dress in uniforms, Martin hoped to visibly demonstrate his desire for a respectable rink. The management always wore tuxedos, remembers daughter Marjorie, who also worked on the floor as a professional skating instructor. The floor staff wore white gloves and fitted red uniforms custom tailored, as well as white hats with dark rims for the men,

Fred Martin, far right, and son Bob Martin, far left, with the professional skating instructors between them, around 1940. From left to right, Joseph Parchem, Vera Wilson, George Brett, Lou Uhley, Jesse Bell, Marjorie Martin McLauchlen, and Earl "Mickey" Dunn.

Of the thirty-two staff members in 1938, seven were women and all four skate boys were African American. By the early 1940s, the Arena Gardens staff grew to nearly forty, with twelve white women working as floor guards and instructors and five black men, again all skate boys. The Arena Gardens staff during the first half of the twentieth century reflected the social structures of Detroit and the nation, with women, excepting Weismuller's widow, absent from management positions, and African American men in service-oriented positions. The staff further reflected those who patronized the rink: white, working class Detroit residents. Few African Americans skated at the Arena Gardens, for though around the time the rink opened Detroit passed a law decreeing it illegal to refuse an African American public service, Detroit remained a heavily divided and racially segregated city throughout the two decades of the Arena Gardens' existence. The Arena Gardens staff and patrons reflected the racially divided city of Detroit in the first half of the twentieth century.

and later a cap for the female employees. The skate boys wore white tailored jackets with dark pants. Warren and Jewell Bowman, who skated at the Arena Gardens following their move to Detroit in the 1940s, always knew where the staff was on the floor because of their uniforms.

The floor staff kept tight control of the crowded Arena Gardens rink floor, where between seven hundred and a thousand people skated each night. Floor guards followed a skating pattern, with a guard in every part of the circumference of the rink and a captain in the center of the rink, observing all. Serving as the well-mannered house police, the uniformed men and women worked to prevent falls and helped people back to their feet when a fall occurred. The Bowmans recall hearing the staff blow their whistles to "warn other skaters to avoid a pileup" following a fall.

If a patron was new to roller skating, Fred Martin called over a professional skating instructor to assist the beginner. The instructor led the novice skater into the 4,000 square foot practice rink, found next to the club locker and dressing rooms. Located near the back of the rink, an entire wall of the practice room was mirrored to assist skaters practicing their movements. The teaching staff provided instruction on how to skate and the fundamentals of skate dancing. By 1941, the Arena Gardens employed fifteen professional skaters to instruct patrons and members of the clubs. The instructors taught all aspects of skating, though the greatest demand was for skate dancing and recreational skating.

While realizing most people roller skated primarily for amusement and relaxation, the Arena Gardens management recommended private, half hour lessons for those skaters who wished to continually improve their skating. Few people, the management believed, skated so well or

Rose Martin wearing the summer Arena Gardens floor staff uniform in 1946, left, and the winter uniform, right, in 1950.

The Arena Gardens practice rink in the early 1940s before mirrors were installed on the walls.

efficiently that they saw their own faults and could then correct them. The Arena Gardens encouraged private lessons and classes, and made sure the skating professionals kept abreast of changes in roller skating to offer tips or answer any questions. If a roller skater decided to take a private lesson, they could sign up at the cost of one dollar per hour in the 1930s. The price for a private lesson increased in the 1940s to two and a half dollars and stayed at this price throughout the early 1950s.

In addition, the Arena Gardens offered classes on various nights of the week before the regular skating session. The classes cost only the admission charge to the rink, which in 1942 cost fifty cents for Arena Gardens Skating Club members and sixty cents for guests. Fred Martin's own children often instructed the classes, with eldest son Bob Martin organizing the first dance skating class in Detroit in January 1936.

Marge Martin McLauchlen instructing the Arena Gardens Junior Figure Skating Club in the early 1940s.

Marjorie and Bob Martin taught the beginner classes on Wednesday nights, which Marjorie recalls "drew adults from all over the city." Their classes, which began when the rink opened, taught thousands of Detroiters to dance on roller skates. Louise Silver, an avid skater at the rink, recalls the Arena Gardens as "the place to learn" how to roller skate.

Marjorie Martin also instructed children on how to roller skate after her father approved of her idea to conduct a class. At twenty-two, Marjorie began instructing children on Saturday mornings along with her younger sister, Rose, then barely sixteen. Beginning with a class of only seven children, Marjorie and Rose proved so popular that registration for the class quickly rose to over two hundred. Peter Breniser recalls attending the Saturday morning classes. Traveling on streetcars with his mother and siblings, Breniser recalls long rides in order to practice with Marjorie and Rose, their instruction proved so worthwhile.

Elsbeth Muller, one of the skating instructors at the Arena Gardens, demonstrates as three year-old Denise Blavatt, in the arms of her mother Rose Martin Blavatt, observe in early 1953. Also watching are some of Muller's pupils, from left, Florence Weigel, Peggy Reid, Joe Slavik, and Betty Hyslop. One of the most famous skating instructors, Elsbeth Muller did not begin roller skating until the late 1930s, when, after watching a performance at the Arena Gardens, she switched from ice to roller skating.

What to Wear to the Rink

Because many viewed roller skating as a social activity from the 1930s through the 1950s, people often wore the same clothing to skate in as they wore to go get ice cream afterwards. Dress regulations for both men and women also stipulated what they could and could not wear to the rink to create the appearance of harmony, and to attract a higher class of clientele. A group of skaters about to begin the grand march provide an example of what people wore in 1938 when they went roller skating at the Arena Gardens.

CHAPTER THREE
A P P R O P R I A T E   A T T I R E

In order to roller skate at the Arena Gardens, Fred Martin required appropriate dress. Attendants who enforced the dress code received special training on explaining to patrons how much more pleasant roller skating was when everyone dressed neatly. Fred Martin often personally enforced the dress code, stopping people from going out onto the floor if inappropriately dressed. "Mr. Martin was very emphatic about his dress code," Warren and Jewell Bowman recall. Martin enforced the dress code in order to keep the crowd appearance from becoming gaudy or unkempt, for Martin believed crowds that dressed poorly behaved rowdily. Margaret Walker agreed with Fred Martin, recalling that the "dress requirements made skating sessions very orderly."

Martin's insistence on a dress code for patrons at the Arena Gardens constitutes the most visible example of his desire to overturn the unsavory reputation of roller rinks with the general public in the 1930s. By insisting that patrons dress formally, as they would to other social events, Martin appealed to the propriety of his patrons. By insisting on a certain level of civility and respect, exemplified in the formal dress requirements, Martin achieved a respectable and safe environment for working and middle class Americans to meet and socialize with each other.

Acceptable attire for women meant a dress or skirt that reached the knees, never slacks, riding breaches, or beach pajamas. Louise Silver remembers that the club locker room patron would not allow the female skaters to leave the locker room until she checked the length of the skirt. While a decade earlier the skirt had to fall to the knee, by the early 1950s acceptable skirt lengths rose. "The skirt had to be below the tip of the second finger when the arms were dropped to the side," recalls

No. D

No. E

A white metallic sophisticated skating dress with button trimmed front.
Circular skirt and three-quarter
length sleeves lined with powder
blue. Side and back zipper.
Sizes 12, 14, 16, 18.   **$19 50**

Two-piece velveteen wool plaid out-
fit. Peter Pan collar, plaid buttons
to match full plaid skirt. Taffeta
lined.
Sizes 12, 14, 16, 18.   **$16 50**

Buying Dresses
An ad from the *Skating Review* magazine in January 1941, for roller skating dresses. While some department stores sold skating dresses, typically designers created these dresses with ice skaters in mind. Subsequently, designers made skating dresses out of heavy material to keep the outdoor ice skater warm. Roller skaters, however, desired dresses made of lighter materials but with the cut of a skating dress to provide for easier movement. By the early 1940s, women seeking roller skating dresses had the option of sewing the dress themselves, mail-ordering, or going to a department store and buying one directly off the rack. The fashion industry also responded to the needs of women roller skaters by developing and marketing whole outfits: the "skaterina," a dress with a full shirred bodice, full circular skirt, and a matching set of bloomers, sold for about three dollars in 1940.

Silver. "No one skated in too short a skirt!"

No woman skated in shorts, either. Peter Breniser, who skated at the Arena Gardens in the 1940s before he enlisted in the armed forces during World War II, recalls an instance when the strict dress code expelled two skaters. Breniser remembers two girls from Cleveland who, although they "knew all the dances" were nonetheless "asked to leave because they had on shorts." Breniser and his friends tried to intercede "but to no avail." No matter how well they roller skated, their inappropriate dress barred them from the Arena Gardens.

While skirt lengths largely set what women could wear, the seasons regulated the dress code for men. Because the Arena Gardens had no air conditioning, between the first of May and the first of October men wearing polos or sport shirts, "if not extreme," were allowed to skate. In the winter, however, men wearing suspenders, sweaters, jackets or non-military uniforms failed the dress code. Men could wear a suit, though they could only remove the coat providing they also wore an "unobtrusively colored" shirt and tie. Rose Martin remembers that her father rented his ties to men not wearing one who desired to skate. Martin loaned out his ties for twenty-five cents or the tie-less man could leave his identification, returned to him when he returned the tie, Rose recalls.

The management of the Arena Gardens believed such stringent dress codes created a better atmosphere at the rink, and they often thanked their patrons for adhering to it. In the January 1951 Arena Gardens Roller Skating Club newsletter, the management stated their pride for the "Arena skaters whom have generously assisted in making our club, the Arena Gardens Roller Skating Club of Detroit, outstanding by following dress rules." Through the duration of its existence, the Arena Gardens forbade casual dress, a rule which in 1951 covered T-shirts, shorts, "ultra-short skirts," dungarees, Levi's, or "any type of working clothes, collarless shirts, or sweaters." As a civil social activity, Martin expected his patrons to dress accordingly.

Marjorie Martin outside the Arena Gardens in the 1940s wearing a dress made specifically for roller skating.

Gail Locke standing in the women's locker room at the Arena Gardens in 1950.

Jesse Bell, near left, Earl King behind the counter, and Fred Martin assist two women in selecting a good roller skate from the skate shop.

CHAPTER FOUR

THE SKATE SHOP

Many roller skaters did not own their skates during this era of the roller rink. To accommodate these patrons, the Arena Gardens created a skate rental room. Prior to 1941, the Arena Gardens rented for ten cents clamp-on roller skates, which attached to a skater's leather shoes. By the early 1940s, however, the Arena switched to renting roller skates with boots attached. Staffed with men knowledgeable about roller skates, the Arena Gardens management made certain the 1,500 pairs of house skates remained in good condition for renters.

The Arena Gardens skate shop occupied a small room just off the main entrance lobby with display windows facing Woodward Avenue. The skate shop sold roller skates starting in 1945, with sizes for children, women, and men in stock. One of the first rinks in the United States to open a sales store, the Arena Gardens installed a fitting room for those wishing to buy their own pair of skates. In 1944, the average price for a pair of skates fell to around fifteen dollars, and over half of roller skaters chose to buy their own skates. Sales associates fitted the boots to the customer's foot, an advantage over the earlier method of buying skates when one mail ordered them and hoped they fit when they arrived. The idea of the shop proved enormously popular and profitable; in any given year, the shop sold three thousand

Eddie Martin in the skate shop maintenance room, 1940.

Rose Martin with a customer in the skate shop in 1946.

pairs of roller skates. Moreover, Earl King and Eddie Martin, Fred Martin's brother, managers of the Arena Gardens skate shop, maintained skates owned by roller skaters. Thousands of Detroit roller skaters came to rely on the department to keep their skates in working order. By 1940, the skate shop also sold skating fashions alongside the roller skates, supplying women with dresses for skating practice or sessions. The average price for the skating outfits ran around ten dollars, with some women spending up to sixty. The skate shop's expansive inventory included boots, skating accessories, skate cases, and men's as well as women's clothing.

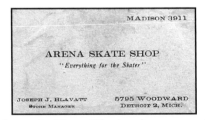

Joseph Blavatt's business card that states the shop that has "Everything for the Skater."

Fred Martin at the skate shop cash register in 1946.

During the summer of 1938, the refreshment counter underwent a complete change. After the renovation, the counter may be classed as one of the finest and most complete.

CHAPTER FIVE
THE REFRESHMENT COUNTER

While the most popular feature about the Arena Gardens remained the rink, the refreshment counter arguably came in a close second. The great service and good food made the counter a popular place to visit while at the rink. Rose Martin recalls working at the counter with her brother Roland for many hours. Nothing, Rose remembers, was ever pre-mixed. Her father, who seemingly directed everything at the Arena Gardens, requested two scoops of ice cream for each sundae, with a topping and a cherry. Along with sundaes, the counter served malteds, milk shakes, Boston coolers, soft drinks made with simple syrup, and hot dogs with hand cut buns. Warren and Jewell Bowman called the Arena Gardens milk shakes the "best ever." One staffer of the counter tested all the black cows he made to make sure they were "just right" before he served them.

The popular refreshment counter underwent a complete make-over in 1938, adding marble and shiny metal to cool drinks and hot dogs. The Bowmans recall greatly enjoying the comfortable coolness of the refreshment counter with the swivel bar stools. According to Rose Martin, the new refreshment counter made a large enough profit to pay for all of the expenses of the entire rink each month.

Taking a break from roller skating, a group gathers at the refreshment counter. Notice the men are all wearing suits.

Russell Bice with Marjorie Martin, who often accompanied him at the organ.

CHAPTER SIX

G R A N D   O R G A N   M U S I C

An absolute essential to a roller rink, music played a key part in the popularity of the Arena Gardens. During the original renovation in 1935, Martin and Weismuller installed a manual three console Wurlitzer Pipe Organ. This theatre-style pipe organ acted as a complete orchestra, with trumpets, horns, and a full compliment of drums, chimes, and bells, but it needed an organist. Nine months after he started playing at the Arena Gardens, Russell Bice recalled the first time he played the Wurlitzer. "On my first touch of the keys I was almost knocked off my feet," Bice remembered. "In all of my born days I had never played on such an instrument as this." The organ, he recalled, "seemed to have a very sensitive touch with tremendous snap and volume, yet retaining beautiful expression." Even more popular than the organ itself was the man who played it for eighteen years, Russell Bice.

Seeking to hire an organist during the rush of opening the rink in 1935, Martin and Weismuller called the American Federation of Musicians to inquire about an organist for the rink. Shortly afterwards, organists, unable to find employment in movie theaters beginning to install sound systems, swamped the Arena Gardens with applications. After trying out several organists, many of whom did not know how to play for roller skaters, Bice auditioned and won the position after playing for barely fifteen minutes. Bice began at the Arena Gardens in November, a month after the rink opened. Originally an organist for movie theaters, Bice expressed his wish in 1939 that he could "remain at the Arena forever."

Indeed, Russell Bice remained with the Arena Gardens for the duration of its existence, a rarity in the rink business. After spending the first three years at the rink, many noted that few organists stayed with a rink for so long a time. Easily the most recognized person who worked at the Arena Gardens aside from the Martin family, Russell Bice "was a favorite of all skaters," recall Warren and Jewell Bowman.

Bice often looked "down at the skaters from the organ loft at the right side of the Arena," watching the skaters as he played. Mirrors placed above the console also allowed Bice to watch the skaters while he played up on his loft. The Bowmans remember always knowing when the skating sessions were about to start up "because Russell could be seen climbing up the ladder to the console." Marjorie Martin, who sometimes accompanied Bice at the organ with her singing, remembers that the rink she grew up in "sparkled with great music by Russell Bice." Similarly, Louise Silver could never forget Bice at the organ. "And oh, how he could play!" According to Silver, his renditions of 'Green Dolphin Street,' a tango, and 'Poinciana,' "brought out the best in every skater in the rink."

Russell Bice at the organ in the loft.

Margaret Williams Walker holding her trophy after winning the Novice Ladies Figures Championship in 1943. Fred Martin is standing directly behind her and next to Fred H. Freeman, the third President of the RSROA.

CHAPTER SEVEN
SERIOUS SKATERS:
THE ARENA GARDENS ROLLER SKATING CLUBS

While recreational roller skaters frequented the rink and joined the Arena Gardens Roller Skating Club, avid skaters also used the resources of the rink to further their knowledge of the sport by joining specific clubs. The year after the Arena Gardens opened, a dozen committed roller skaters formed the Detroit Fancy Skating Club. That same year, skaters age four to fourteen could join the Children's Safety Skating Club. By 1942, a resident of Detroit could choose from seven clubs at the Arena Gardens.

The Detroit Fancy Skating Club quickly became one of the most renowned skating clubs in the United States, producing a host of champions. With the dedicated work of Bob Martin, who taught them all, skaters from the Arena Gardens dominated the first artistic roller skating championships in 1939, winning every title except dance. By 1940, the club boasted that its members "have captured more places in competition than any other club." Skating figures, dance, or pairs, children, teenagers, and adults received instruction from Bob Martin, the club pro,

Michigan's state speed skating champions for 1941 at the Arena Gardens, from left: Ray Gene Bell, Dale Godfrey, Verna Picton, Harry Lindbergh, Dorothy Law, Roy Booth, and Eleanor King. All were from the Arena Gardens except Godfrey and Booth.

The four Arena Gardens Figure Skating Club members who swept the United States National Championships in 1952. From left, Sandra Krygier, Junior Ladies Figures; Gail Locke, International Ladies Figures; Nancy Kromis, Senior Ladies Figures; Carolyn Green, Novice Ladies Figures.

Jack Holcomb, Detroit Junior Boys Speed Champion for 1938, Ed Theiner, the 1937 United States National Speed Champion, and Millie Mulligan, the 1937 Detroit Junior Girls Speed Skating Champion at the Arena Gardens in 1938.

and the other professional instructors. Dedicated roller skaters saw the value of the club, and of Bob Martin's teaching excellence. Some, like Melva Block, traveled thirty miles from Romulus Township to Detroit to participate, becoming a member when she was fourteen.

As a direct result of the excellence of the Detroit Fancy Skating Club, the Arena Gardens quickly became a "major hub" for those who wished to compete, recalls Margaret Williams Walker. Outsiders regularly visited to observe and take notes to share with their skaters back home. Walker, a figures champion from the club, remembers "practicing and people watching us for hours." In addition to people from other rinks, the men who wrestled at the Arena Gardens on Tuesday evenings also observed the club skaters. According to Walker, "wrestlers quite often hung out and watched skaters practice, leaning against the front railing" of the stands surrounding the rink. Walker recalls the very large club possessing "scads of talent."

Speed skaters in Detroit also learned from professionals Jesse Bell and Eddie Martin at the Arena Gardens upon joining the Speed Skating Club. Meetings of the speed club focused upon race drills and instruction classes, and the club produced a number of champions. Members met on Sunday mornings, before the rink opened for regular skating sessions, to practice under the direction of Jesse Bell, the rink's Speed Club professional.

The Children's Safety Skating Club, founded In the fall of 1936, met on Saturday afternoons. Over three hundred children became members within the first month. According to the Arena Gardens management, skating on Saturday afternoons proved so popular that given the choice a child often opted to skate at the Arena Gardens over attending the movies. Children learned skate dancing, like the adults, but also participated in games and races. Arena Gardens parents liked the club, for it promoted fairness and safety, and it allowed their children someplace safe off the street to roller skate.

Later, in the early 1940s, children who graduated from the Children's Safety Skating Club by turning fourteen moved to the Sunday Matinee Club, designed for teenagers still too young to skate with adults. The Arena Gardens also set aside time on Sunday afternoons for teenagers because Detroit's juvenile curfew prohibited anyone under the age of sixteen to be out in the evenings. Fred Martin followed the curfew closely, forbidding even his own children, Rose Martin recalls, from skating past ten.

The Skating Vanities
Many of the talented roller skaters at the Arena Gardens went on to perform in the traveling roller skating extravaganza, the Skating Vanities. Begun in 1942 by a former boxing promoter, the show became a huge hit at first domestically and then internationally after it went abroad in 1948. Melva Block, Douglas Breniser, Anne Manion, William Martin, and Nancy Lee Parker, to name a few, all left Detroit to tour with the show. Featured above, Douglas Breniser took a starring role next to the most famous of the Skating Vanities skaters, Gloria Nord.

A photograph collage of the Arena Gardens support for the war effort, bottom left clockwise: a flag hanging in the rink, the Honors Board, a Victory poster, Fred Martin holding keys donated for materials, and an Arena employee selling War Bonds and Stamps.

CHAPTER EIGHT
WORLD WAR II
& THE ARENA GARDENS

When America went to war in 1941, it disrupted the lives of an entire nation. Increased mobilization of the armed forces occurred rapidly; within a year, hundreds of thousands of American men between the ages of eighteen and thirty-nine enlisted. More than sixteen million Americans ultimately served in the armed forces during the Second World War. Before the war ended, over 600,000 men and women from Michigan served in the armed services, with Detroit supplying approximately one third of that number. Few families in Detroit remained directly unaffected by the war by not having a son or daughter, cousin or uncle, in the armed forces.

The Arena Gardens sent many young skaters to war, including Fred Martin's son Roland. An Honor Board at the Arena Gardens commemorated those enlisted men and women who during peace time skated at the rink. The Arena Gardens Roller Skating Club dedicated the 1941-1942 Year Book to those "who have laid aside their skates to help defend America." Skaters remaining stateside learned about their friends in the service from the *Detroit Roller Skater*, the newsletter of the Arena Gardens Roller Skating Club. Many former Arena

Fred Martin giving a presentation in front of the Arena Gardens Honor Board during World War II.

Skaters enjoying a break from the war by roller skating at the Arena Gardens. From left to right, an unidentified enlisted man, Virginia Mount, Lloyd Young, Ann Manion, Bruce Towle, Louise Moore, and Alden Sibley.

Gardens skaters wrote to their old rink to let them know how the military was treating them and also to ask for news of their friends at the rink. Arena Gardens skaters who remained in Detroit during the war, including Fred Martin, wrote to fellow skaters overseas in the armed forces.

While many who enlisted from the Arena Gardens received a furlough home and returned to the rink of their earlier days, Fred Martin let in every uniformed soldier on leave as guests during the war. By September 1943, Martin estimated that over seventeen thousand members of the armed forces had skated as guests of the Arena Gardens Roller Skating Club. The management supported the free admission, feeling that "roller skating is beneficial to the MORALE of men in the service." Moreover, by admitting soldiers as guests, the club felt they showed "our appreciation to these men who unselfishly are giving their all in defense of our beloved country."

At home, Americans helped in the war effort in a variety of ways.

Advertisement for a benefit for the women in the service at the Arena Gardens.

Many men and women in Detroit worked for one of the "Big Three" auto manufactures, all of which converted to war production of airplanes and tanks. Activated in 1941, the Chrysler Tank Arsenal in Detroit quickly became the nation's largest defense plant. The last civilian

Pontiac rolled off the assembly line in the early spring of 1942, with Ford, Plymouth, Studebaker, and Packard having already ended their civilian manufacturing. As Detroit manufacturers converted to war production, many Arena skaters went to work in the factories. Dorothy Law and Louise Moore worked as plant messengers in the early years of the war, delivering messages on roller skates. War work brought an economic boom to Detroit, awarding the metropolitan area contracts totaling well over twelve billion dollars by 1944.

Americans also helped in the war effort through purchasing Victory War Bonds. The bonds were sold on street corners, in grocery stores, in banks, and at roller rinks. In 1943, the members of the Arena Gardens Roller Skating Club proudly received a "100% War Bond Buying Certificate." Club members earned the certificate through buying war bonds at the rate of at least ten percent of their earnings.

Along with purchasing war bonds, Americans stateside underwent rationing of many items. Food, gasoline, and household appliances made of metal all were rationed in order that the materials could go toward war production. Skates and skate parts also become limited as skate manufacturers converted to war production. Due to the scarcity of leather, the Arena Gardens skate shop switched to canvas boots during the war. Though rationing limited the availability of skates, boots, and attachments, the Arena Gardens skate shop promised to "do our best to serve" during the "emergency" while such equipment was deferred for the duration of the war.

Kenny Chase and fellow member of the Arena Gardens Figures Skating Club Norma Jeanne Wescher skating in the late 1930s. Chase joined the armed forces and died during World War II. An accomplished skater, the Chase Waltz was later named in his honor.

Fred Martin presenting money for the purchase of an iron lung to the Mayor of Detroit, Louis Mariani, in the early 1950s. From left, Patsy Martino, Marilyn Adams, Bill Pate, Mr. Martino, Martin, Mariani, Jim Miller, Earl King, Sandy Krygier, and Carolyn Green in front of the club desk.

CHAPTER NINE

A NEW WAR AFTER

WORLD WAR II:

DETROIT ROLLER SKATERS AGAINST POLIO

Following the Second World War, Detroit and the Arena Gardens welcomed home their veterans, celebrating the end of the bloody conflict. Rose Martin recalls standing in front of the Arena Gardens on VE Day and watching cars line Woodward Avenue bumper to bumper, with people standing on the running boards celebrating the end of the war. Americans, however, soon began fighting a new, domestic war. The staff and members of the Arena Gardens clubs, like millions of Americans, helped in the postwar crusade against one of the most feared diseases in the nation: polio.

Prior to the 1930s, the majority of Americans associated polio with dirt, poor hygiene, and urban slums. But during the 1920s and 1930s, with increasingly severe epidemics striking the middle class, Americans came to understand that polio favored cleanliness, and occurred chiefly among children and young adults who had been protected in early infancy from polio infection. Scientists seeking to further understand the disease concluded that clean, protected middle class children tended to have lower immunity levels against polio than poor children, who often contracted the disease during infancy and thus acquired immunity. This knowledge, along with the activism of Franklin Roosevelt, the future President of the United States who contracted polio during a family vacation in 1927, further eroded the misconceptions and stigma surrounding the debilitating disease.

In 1937, five years after his election to the presidency, Roosevelt

Program from the first RSROA benefit exhibition.

helped found the National Foundation for Infantile Paralysis. The foundation conducted paralysis research and assisted families with medical expenses. With the effects of polio intimately visible, millions of Americans came to view the foundation as their private charity, and worked diligently raising money to assist in the battle against polio.

Roller skaters at the Arena Gardens, largely due to the work of Fred Martin, likewise became actively involved in the fight against polio. Martin helped form and chaired a Roller Skating Rink Operators Association branch of the National Foundation for Infantile Paralysis in 1943. Martin referred to the charity as the "personal and private charity of everyone connected with the roller sport." In an

Program from the second RSROA benefit exhibition at Madison Square Garden.

effort to support the charity, Martin helped organize the Roller Skating Rink Operators Association roller skating exhibition benefit held at Madison Square Garden in New York City on February 16, 1944. Martin and other members of the association assembled the largest number of roller skaters ever for a benefit exhibition. Over five hundred skaters participated in the exhibition, a number that included many Arena Gardens club members. The association's benefit raised over $10,000 for the National Foundation for Infantile Paralysis. Pete Martin, who covered the event for the *Saturday Evening Post,* called

Fred Martin presenting an iron lung to the City of Detroit in 1951.

the polio benefit the "coming of age" of roller skating.

Martin urged "every man and woman associated with the roller sport" to support the foundation's battle against polio and he worked diligently toward that goal. At home, Fred Martin and club members organized their own benefit shows for years following the Madison Square Garden extravaganza. With the slogan "we skate today so that some unfortunate child may walk tomorrow," proceeds from the Arena Gardens Roller Skating Club 1952-1953 Skating Revue purchased an iron lung, used by people with polio who were often unable to breathe without the aid of the machine. The Arena Garden skaters continued to skate for the benefit of the National Foundation for Infantile Paralysis, by then called the March of Dimes, until the rink closed its doors.

The last photograph of the Arena Gardens.

CHAPTER TEN

CLOSING DETROIT'S
BIG RED & GOLD DOORS

With the end of the war, and men and women returning home, Detroit's economy and population boomed. In 1950, the population of Detroit proper reached nearly two million, and the metropolitan Detroit population exceeded three million when counting the outlying areas. Jobs in Detroit's motor industry were plentiful. With money in their pockets, low interest rates, and easy down payments through the GI Bill, owning a home became a feasible dream for millions of young married couples across the United States and in Detroit. In 1950 alone, over one million homes were built in this country, nearly all of them in suburbs surrounding metropolitan cities. In 1955, *House and Garden* magazine called the move to suburbia "the national way of life." In order to accommodate its population moving to the suburbs, Detroit constructed new roads and established freeways leading to the growing outskirts of the city.

The Arena Gardens sat in one of the areas scheduled for the construction of an expressway. Though remaining strong and profitable, with upwards of twenty-five thousand people roller skating a year, in the late spring of 1953 the Arena Gardens closed forever. The rink shut the bright red and gold doors for the last time on Sunday, May 3, 1953. One Detroit newspaper called the closing of the Arena Gardens that Sunday "the end of an era in American roller skating." Construction began shortly after May 3 on the future Edsel Ford Expressway.

The city lamented the loss "of one of the oldest sport sanctuaries," and some wondered whether another rink equal to the Arena Gardens would rise elsewhere. Asked by the *Detroit News* whether he planned to build another rink, Fred Martin stated that he felt the expense too high,

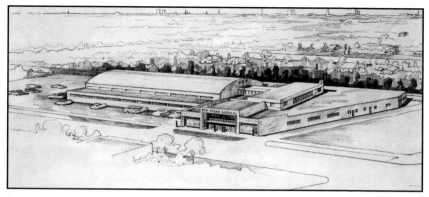

Preliminary description for the New Arena Gardens never built as designed by Lyle Zisler and Associates. The proposed new rink entrance is through a large, high ceilinged lobby lined with display cases and bulletin panels. The lobby leads past the ticket-taker openings into the Foyer which is the center of off-rink activity. On three sides of the Foyer is the Dairy Bar, the Rink Retail Store, Management Office, Club Desk and Check Room. The rink floor is 80' x 185' with a vaulted acoustical ceiling and a balcony with an organ for live music. The total specified was estimated at $631,500.00.

placing the cost above a quarter of a million dollars to duplicate the Arena Gardens. "I guess I'll go fishing," Martin concluded.

Many mourned the loss of Detroit's "capital rink," including Martin's staff of forty, several of whom had worked at the Arena Gardens since the opening of the rink in 1935 with Martin. Martin's children, who grew up with the Arena Gardens, were also affected. Marjorie recalls the closing as a "very sad occasion." Her brother Roland called the closing "comparable to a family break-up." Rose, to whom "that rink and Dad" made up her life, stated more than forty years after the Arena Gardens closed, that she still remains affected by its closing.

Those who patronized the Arena Gardens remember it fondly. Louise Silver remembers the Arena Gardens as "the place to go, it was the place to meet friends." William Martin remembers the "wonderful years" when he skated at the Arena Gardens, as well as the "many friends I made." Many people, Marjorie believes, "lost their focal point" when the rink closed, "as the Arena had been a gathering place for so many years." Its closure "left a hole in many people's lives." Her brother,

Roland, calls the closing of the Arena the "end of an era" in Detroit. Asked why one rink's closing could have affected so many lives, Roland Martin responded that the Arena Gardens attracted people. The Arena Gardens, Roland recalls, "like the line from the theme song of the television series 'Cheers,' was a place where everybody knew your name."

Part of an envelope used at the Arena Gardens, "Where Roller Skating is a Pleasure."

BIBLIOGRAPHY

Primary Sources

"Boom in Roller Skating Echoes Over the Nation with Cleveland Setting Pace in Experts Tourney," *Newsweek (May* 5, 1941): 48.

"Fun on Wheels," *Time* (November 25, 1940): 64-65.

"History on Wheels," *Time* (March 27, 1944): 90, 93.

Martin, Pete, "They're Taking the Kinks out of Rinks," *The Saturday Evening Post* (May 13, 1944): 26+.

Michigan: A Guide to the Wolverine State Writers' Program of the Work Project Administration, compilers (New York: Oxford University Press, 1941).

"Roller-Skate Dancing Starts a Bloomers Fad," *Life* (July 8, 1940): 68.

National Museum of Roller Skating Archives:
    The Arena Gardens Collection
        Arena Gardens Roller Skating Club year books, 1936-1942
        Rose Martin, letter to George Pickard, December 24, 1979
        "We Are Proud," Arena Gardens Roller Skating Club of Detroit newsletter, (January 1951): 1.
        "Martin Preps Final Curtain for Arena," (April 25, 1953):
        Ken Williams, "Little Citadel of Sports, Arena Gardens, Closes its Doors Sunday,"

    Letters to author, Arena Gardens Correspondence
        Warren and Jewell Bowman, August 13, 1997
        Peter C. Breniser, November 8, 1997
        Roland A. Martin, August 15, 1997
        Rose Martin, July 10, 1997
        Rose Martin, July 31, 1997
        William L. Martin, August 26, 1997
        Marjorie McLauchlen, August 13, 1997
        Louise Silver, August 26, 1997
        Margaret Williams Walker, tape to author, November 1997

Periodicals
> *Skating Review* (February 1942)
> *Skating Review* (March 1943)
> *Skating Review* (Arena Gardens Issue, 1943)
> "Requiem for a Rink," *Skating News* (April 1953) 3.

USA Roller Skating Coaches Hall of Fame Collection
Data sheet on Robert Martin

Secondary Sources

Braden, Donna R., *Leisure and Entertainment in America* (Detroit: Henry Ford Museum and Greenfield Village, 1988).

Brooslin, Michael W., *Report on the Origins and Early History of the Roller Skating RSROA* (Lincoln: National Museum of Roller Skating, 1983).

Casdorph, Paul D., *Let the Good Times Roll: Life at Home in America During World War II* (New York: Paragon House, 1989).

Conot, Robert, *American Odyssey* (New York: William Morrow and Co., 1974).

Fischer, Clause S., "Changes in Leisure Time Activities, 1890-1940," *Journal of Social History* 27 no. 3 (1994): 453-475.

"The Fred Martin Story," *Skate* (February 1959): 10.

Glazer, Sidney, *Detroit: A Study in Urban Development* (New York: Bookman Associates, Inc., 1965).

Heide, Robert and John Gilman, *Home Front America: Popular Culture of the World War Two Era* (San Francisco: Chronicle Books, 1995).

Lewis, David H., *Roller Skating for Gold* (London: The Scarecrow Press, Inc., 1997).

Lutz, William W., *The News of Detroit: How a Newspaper and a City Grew Together* (Boston: Little, Brown, and Co., 1973).

Mandell, Richard D., *Sport: A Cultural History* (New York: Columbia University Press, 1984).

Our American Century: The American Dream, The 50s Editors of Time-Life Books, eds. (Richmond: Time-Life Books, 1998).

Pound, Arthur, *Detroit: Dynamic City* (New York: D. Appleton-Century Co., 1940).

Rogers, Naomi, *Dirt and Disease: Polio Before FDR* (New Brunswick: Rutgers University Press, 1992).

Shogun, Robert and Tom Craig, *The Detroit Race Riot: A Study in Violence* (Philadelphia: Chilton Books, 1964).

Spears, Betty and Richard A. Swanson, *History of Sport and Physical Education in the United States* 3rd ed., (Dubuque: Wm. C. Brown Publishers, 1988).

Turner, Jim in collaboration with Michael Zaidman, *The History of Roller Skating* (Lincoln: National Museum of Roller Skating, 1997).

Webber, Sarah, "Follies on Wheels: The Skating Vanities, 1940-1955," *Historical Roller Skating Overview* (February/March 1998): 3-5.

— "A Grand Show for an Even Grander Cause: The 1944 Roller Skating Rink Operators Association Benefit Exhibition for the Infantile Paralysis Foundation," *Historical Roller Skating Overview* (August/ September 1997): 3-5.

—"Roller Skating through the Second World War," *Historical Roller Skating Overview* (June/July 1997): 3-6.

—"1900-1997: A Century of Rinking Across the United States," *Historical Roller Skating Overview* (April/May 1998): 3-7.

Wise, Nancy Baker and Christy Wise, *A Mouthful of Rivets: Women at Work in World War II* (San Francisco: Jossey-Bass Publishers, 1994).

Wolf, Cathy, "75 Years in Business, Basic Operation Still Unchanged," *Rinksider* (May 1981): 22A.

Woodford, Frank B. and Arthur M. Woodford, *All Our Yesterdays: A Brief History of Detroit* (Detroit: Wayne State University Press, 1969).

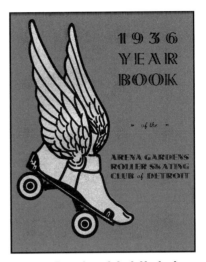

Year Books highlighting the year of 1936 above and 1937-8 below.